Purity

by Thomas Bradshaw

SAMUEL FRENCH

FOUNDED 1830

NEW YORK HOLLYWOOD LONDON TORONTO

SAMUELFRENCH.COM

ISBN 978-0-573-65011-6   Printed in U.S.A.   #17853

MUSIC USE NOTE

Licensees are solely responsible for obtaining formal written permission from copyright owners to use copyrighted music in the performance of this play and are strongly cautioned to do so. If no such permission is obtained by the licensee, then the licensee must use only original music that the licensee owns and controls. Licensees are solely responsible and liable for all music clearances and shall indemnify the copyright owners of the play and their licensing agent, Samuel French, Inc., against any costs, expenses, losses and liabilities arising from the use of music by licensees.

IMPORTANT BILLING AND CREDIT
REQUIREMENTS

All producers of *PURITY* must give credit to the Author of the Play in all programs distributed in connection with performances of the Play, and in all instances in which the title of the Play appears for the purposes of advertising, publicizing or otherwise exploiting the Play and/or a production. The name of the Author *must* appear on a separate line on which no other name appears, immediately following the title and *must* appear in size of type not less than fifty percent of the size of the title type.

PURITY was first produced in January 2007 at Performance Space 122 in Manhattan. The Director was Yehuda Duenyas with Set design by Clint Ramos, Lighting Design by Ben Kato, Costumes by Jessica Gaffney. The production was Stage Managed by Michelle Chang. The cast was as follows:

VERNON. . . . . James Scruggs
DAVE. . . . . Daniel Manley
CARL . . . . Albert Christmas
LISA . . . . Alexa Scott-Flaherty
MICHELLE. . . . . .Kate Benson
ECUADORIAN MAN/GENIE . . . . Spencer Barros
MARIA . . . . Jenny Seastone Stern

Purity was developed in the Soho Repertory Theater
Writer/Director Lab.

CHARACTERS

VERNON - 40, An African-American Professor at a prestigious university.

DAVE - 40, White, Vernon's best friend and the Chairman of the English Department.

LISA - Late thirties, White, Vernon's wife and a neurosurgeon.

MICHELLE - Early forties, White, Dave's wife and a powerful lawyer.

CARL - Early thirties, African-American, A professor in the English department.

ECUADORIAN MAN

MARIA - Ecuadorian Man's daughter.

GENIE

Ecuadorian man and the Genie can be double cast.

Maria must be played by an actress who is at least 18 years old.

The setting is New York City, The Present

AUTHOR'S NOTES

All characters should be played with the utmost honesty and sincerity. The irony in the play should be underplayed rather than overplayed at all times. The characters in this play feel that all their actions are completely necessary and unavoidable. The play should be directed in a straightforward and realistic manner.

Scene One

(At rise DAVE is in his office and VERNON ENTERS with bits of vomit on his shirt. VERNON is visibly hung over.)

DAVE. Hey. What's up?

VERNON. I have to go teach in a few minutes.

DAVE. What are you teaching?

VERNON. Wuthering Heights. It's my favorite book.

DAVE. I know. *(Pause.)* What the fuck is on your shirt? It's disgusting.

VERNON. *(Looks at his shirt.)* Oh man. It's vomit. I'm so fucking hung over. I was walking out of the library and I suddenly I got really nauseous, so I ran and threw up into the first garbage can I saw for like five minutes.

DAVE. That sucks dude.

VERNON. The worst part is that two of my students saw me vomiting. It's so embarrassing.

DAVE. It'll be o.k. Just make up something. Say you ate some bad fish or that you have the flu. *(Pause.)* You really look like shit. Let me get you a fresh shirt.

(DAVE goes into his closet and gets VERNON a clean shirt. VERNON changes.)

VERNON. You got something for my hangover?

DAVE. Yeah. *(DAVE goes and pours VERNON a glass of Johnnie Walker Black Label. Then he goes to his desk and takes out a mirror with a pile of cocaine on it.)* This stuff is primo man. It'll blow your mind.

(They both do a line and VERNON drinks his scotch.)

VERNON. Thanks man. I really needed that.
DAVE. You should never teach sober. That's my rule. I thought you would've learned that by now.
VERNON. Is that right? That's a great motto for the chairman of the English department to live by. You should distribute your motto to all the professors in the department. I'm sure the president would love that.

(They both have a good laugh.)

DAVE. Fuck the president. I should be the president. I don't know why the board gave Michael that job.
VERNON. He's got all that money. That's why.
DAVE. Anyway, I'm thinking about tinkering with the English 211 curriculum a little bit.
VERNON. How?
DAVE. I think we should have students read *Jane Eyre* instead of *Wuthering Heights*.
VERNON. Why?
DAVE. My students aren't connecting to *Wuthering Heights* this semester. I've never had much luck getting the students to connect to this novel. I think they'd find it easier to relate to the themes and plot of *Jane Eyre*. *Jane Eyre* really speaks to youth.
VERNON. That's the most retarded thing I've ever heard you say. *Wuthering Heights* is the greatest literary achievement of the

PURITY

nineteenth century. Just because you're an incompetent teacher doesn't mean that *Wuthering Heights* should be taken out of the curriculum.

DAVE. Oh. I see the problem now. I'm incompetent.

VERNON. That's right.

(DAVE playfully punches VERNON in the chest and they playfight. It's a playfight where they're hitting each other pretty hard.)

DAVE. You're the incompetent one! Who threw up in a garbage can in front of his students?

VERNON. Yeah well, you want to fuck Charlotte Bronte.

DAVE. And you want to fuck Emily Bronte. Oh and speaking of fucking, look what I got this week.

(They stop playfighting and DAVE goes and gets some kiddie porn from the drawer of his desk. The pictures are of a ten year old girl having sex with a grown man.)

VERNON. Oh my god. This girl is so hot. Jesus Christ. She's so little. Where did you get these from?

DAVE. My buddy went down to Ecuador and took these pictures himself. Their laws are pretty lax.

VERNON. How old do you think she is?

DAVE. Nine or ten.

VERNON. Dude. We need to go to Ecuador!

DAVE. That's a great idea. But how would we get away from our wives?

VERNON. We'll tell them that there's an English conference down there. We'll tell them that we want some male bonding time. It'll be just like when we were teenagers. Sneaking around, smoking pot in your mom's basement.

PURITY

DAVE. Do you remember the time we were smoking pot in your basement and your dad caught us using his bong?

(They laugh.)

VERNON. He was so pissed.

DAVE. But not about the fact that we were smoking pot. He was pissed about the fact that we were using his bong. You're dad's awesome.

(They laugh.)

VERNON. Those were the good old days. *(Looking at the pictures again.)* She's so little dude. It looks like he's splitting her open. Oh god she's so hot.

DAVE. I know man. I jerked off four times last night. I can't get enough of this little girl.

VERNON. I think I need to jerk off.

DAVE. Go for it. No use torturing yourself.

(DAVE gestures for VERNON to go into the bathroom. VERNON does. DAVE sits down and does some more coke. VERNON re-emerges from the bathroom about a minute and a half later.)

VERNON. Oh my god Dave. That was amazing! Dude. This little girl. Dude. I came so hard that my cum hit me in the face.

DAVE. *(In Disbelief.)* No way!

VERNON. I'm totally serious.

DAVE. Really?

VERNON. Yeah.

DAVE. Wow.

VERNON. We need to go to Ecuador man.

PURITY

DAVE. Are you really serious?

VERNON. I'm sick of masturbating while thinking about little girls. I need the real thing.

DAVE. Let's do it brother.

(They shake hands. VERNON looks at his watch.)

VERNON. Oh shit! I'm late for class.

End Scene

Scene Two

(At rise VERNON is at home when his wife walks in.)

VERNON. How was your day honey?

(They kiss.)

LISA. I think I need to stop doing so much coke.

VERNON. *(Horrified.)* Don't say things like that. I won't let you slander cocaine's good name in my house!

LISA. I'm serious Vernon.

VERNON. *(Hugs her.)* I'm sorry. What happened?

LISA. Well nothing happened. Well actually, I was performing surgery today and couldn't get my hand to stop shaking. I mean, I'm operating on this guy's brain and my hand wouldn't stop shaking!

VERNON. Did everything turn out all right?

LISA. Yeah. But that's a fluke. The brain's so fragile. One slip on my part and that man would've been paralyzed. *(Pause.)* I think that I maybe need to stop using cocaine at work.

VERNON. How do you know it was the cocaine?

LISA. Vernon. It was the fucking cocaine! Okay?

VERNON. *(Hugs her. Gives her a kiss on the forehead.)* I support you no matter what you decide to do.

LISA. Oh who am I kidding? I'll just try to do a little less. I mean, this is the first time this has happened to me.

VERNON. Now that's the spirit! That's the Lisa I know.

(They kiss.)

LISA. How was your day?

VERNON. Dave told me about this English conference that's going to be held in Ecuador.

LISA. Are you going to go?

VERNON. I'm thinking about it.

LISA. We should go! I've always wanted to go to Ecuador. Some vacation time would really do me some good.

VERNON. Well actually, Um. Dave and I were thinking that it would be like a male bonding kind of thing.

LISA. Oh I see. You two want to travel around the world drinking and carousing with the local women. You don't want your wives dragging you down, preventing you from having sex with whores!

(She laughs.)

VERNON. That's not it and you know it. It's just that Dave and I don't get to spend a lot of time alone together anymore. I mean usually when we hang out it's the four of us.

LISA. Oh, so you guys don't like spending time with your wives.

PURITY

I'm sorry. I didn't know we were such a burden to you guys. We who support you two poor English professors. Whose money do you think will be paying for that trip to Ecuador?

VERNON. It's not like that. We just want to have some time alone. It'll be like when we were in high school. Don't you ever want to just hang out with your girlfriends?

LISA. I'm just giving you a hard time. I know exactly what you mean.

VERNON. I love you.

LISA. I love you too.

VERNON. And don't worry. We're not going to carouse with any women.

LISA. You better not.

VERNON. You're the only woman for me. You're so sexy. I love you more that anything in the world.

(They make out as the lights fade to black.)

End Scene

Scene Three

(At rise DAVE, VERNON, and a MAN from Ecuador are drinking and laughing as the lights come up. DAVE and VERNON have flown to Ecuador.)

DAVE. I can't believe you shot yourself in the foot!

ECUADORIAN MAN. I was young! I didn't want to get drafted

into army! Army in Ecuador not a fun place to be!

VERNON. I think what you did makes perfect sense. I've often thought about what I would do if I got drafted.

DAVE. You're way too old to get drafted now! *(They laugh.)* Would you actually shoot yourself in the foot?

VERNON. If it came to that. I'd probably try to convince them that I was gay first.

(More laughing.)

ECUADORIAN MAN. You Americans don't like homosexual. That's good. We Ecuadorians don't like sinful homosexual either.

DAVE. Yeah.

(Awkward pause.)

VERNON. So. Um. You said you have a daughter?

ECUADORIAN MAN. Yes. I hope she never turn out to be homosexual. She is good girl. She is Joy of my life since my wife die.

DAVE. How did your wife die?

ECUADORIAN MAN. Car accident. Four years ago.

VERNON. We're sorry to hear that.

ECUADORIAN MAN. I loved her more than sky and moon.

DAVE. How old is your daughter?

ECUADORIAN MAN. Nine. *(Pause.)*

VERNON. We were wondering whether we could spend some time with your daughter?

ECUADORIAN MAN. Why you want to spend time with my daughter? She have nothing interesting to say. She just little girl.

DAVE. Not to talk to her exactly. I mean we would. We'd give you money.

PURITY

ECUADORIAN MAN. *(Kind of Enraged. ECUADORIAN MAN stands up.)* You want to buy my daughter?!

VERNON. Yeah. Kind of.

(Long silence.)

ECUADORIAN MAN. How much you pay me?

DAVE. How much do you want?

ECUADORIAN MAN. One thousand dollars.

DAVE. Deal.

ECUADORIAN MAN. Let's go to my house. We pack her things. Can I come visit her in America? That's where you take her. Right?

VERNON. Oh. You don't understand. We didn't really mean buy. We meant more like rent.

ECUADORIAN MAN. Oh! You want rent daughter. So you no take her?

VERNON. No. We'd like to rent her for a few hours a day if possible.

ECUADORIAN MAN. How long you be here?

DAVE. One week.

ECUADORIAN MAN. How much you give me to rent daughter for week?

VERNON. Two hundred dollars.

ECUADORIAN MAN. Five hundred dollars.

VERNON. Three hundred dollars.

ECUADORIAN MAN. Five hundred dollars.

VERNON. Deal.

DAVE. So when can we pick her up?

ECUADORIAN MAN. You no pick her up. You rent her at my house.

VERNON. We'd rather pick her up.

ECUADORIAN MAN. No! You rent her at my house. Four hours a day. I work field while you rent. No worry. No one will bother you.

DAVE. Okay.

ECUADORIAN MAN. Come to my house 1pm tomorrow. I live in pink house at end of road. My wife like that color.

End Scene

Scene Four

(At rise DAVE and VERNON have arrived at the ECUADORIAN MAN's house.)

ECUADORIAN MAN. *(Cheerfully.)* Welcome!

VERNON. Thanks.

DAVE. It's good to see you.

ECUADORIAN MAN. Maria. Come down here. You have guests. *(MARIA ENTERS.)* These very nice men have come to spend time with you while I work field. You must do whatever they ask you to. You understand?

MARIA. Yes.

(ECUADORIAN MAN kisses her on the forehead.)

ECUADORIAN MAN. I love you. I see you in a few hours.

MARIA. I love you daddy.

PURITY

(ECUADORIAN MAN EXITS.)

DAVE. Hi Maria. My name's Dave.

MARIA. Hi Dave.

VERNON. And my name is Vernon.

MARIA. Hi Vernon.

DAVE. Where's your room?

MARIA. *(She points.)* Do you want to come play with me?

DAVE. Yeah we'll play soon. Can you go wait for us in there? We need to have an adult conversation. *(She nods her head and goes into her room.)* This is awesome! She's so fucking little!

VERNON. We hit the Jackpot dude!

DAVE. What should we do? Should we take turns or double team her?

VERNON. I think we should take turns. I think double teaming her might traumatize her right now.

DAVE. You're right.

VERNON. We'll play it by ear. She might be ready to be double teamed by the end of the week.

DAVE. Who should go first?

VERNON. I think I should go first.

DAVE. Why do you get to go first?

VERNON. I don't know. It's just what I think.

DAVE. Fine. You can go first. *(VERNON starts to go into her room.)* But you can't fuck her in the ass.

VERNON. What? Why not?

DAVE. If you get to fuck her pussy first, then I should get to fuck her ass first. It's only fair!

VERNON. I don't know.

DAVE. Think of it this way. You're taking her pussy virginity and I'm taking her ass virginity.

VERNON. Okay. Deal. *(Pause.)* Do you have something to read?

DAVE. Yeah. But you won't be in there too long. *(They laugh.)*

(VERNON EXITS into MARIA's room.)

End Scene

Scene Five

(At rise VERNON is in MARIA's room.)

VERNON. Hi Maria. You're very beautiful. Did you know that?

(He's stroking her hair.)

MARIA. My dad tell me that sometime.
VERNON. I've always wanted a little girl like you. *(He kisses her and undresses her. He tries to move her to her bed. She is reluctant.)* Don't worry. I'm not going to hurt you. *(She relents and lies on her bed. VERNON takes off his pants.)* You're going to become a woman now. *(He starts trying to get his penis inside her. She groans as if she's pain.)* It's okay. It always hurts the first time some one loves you. You feel so good Maria. *(He's doing it slowly and sweetly and kissing her face. She pants a little.)* I love you. Divine Maria. You're heaven. *(He ejaculates. He lies with her for a few moments and strokes her hair.)* Now that didn't hurt too much. Did it?
MARIA. No. *(She is crying a little.)* This is love?
VERNON. Yes. Dave and I love you very much. You're a good girl.

(He puts back on his pants and EXITS.)

VERNON. *(Offstage.)* Your turn.

DAVE. *(Offstage.)* How was she.

VERNON. *(Offstage.)* It's indescribable. She's amazing. So tight. Primo man. Do you have some KY?

DAVE. Yeah. *(He enters the room. He takes off his clothes and gets into bed with her.)* Why are you crying? Don't cry. There's nothing to cry about. Now turn over. *(He flips her onto her belly.)* We're going to do something a little different. *(He takes out lubricant and smears it in between her butt cheeks. He then starts to ram his penis into her anus roughly and she screams.)* Yeah. This is going to hurt a little. *(He finally gets it all the way in and starts to pump away furiously without any regard for her. She is crying and screaming uncontrollably.)* This is good for you, you little slut! It'll put hair on your chest. Oh, your little ass pussy feels too good! *(He ejaculates. He puts back on his clothes.)* We'll be back tomorrow. Make sure to look pretty. We're going to be taking pictures.

End Scene

Scene Six

(At rise DAVE has just returned from his trip to Ecuador. He greets his wife MICHELLE.)

DAVE. Hey Honey!

PURITY

MICHELLE. Hi! *(They kiss.)* How was your trip?

DAVE. Fantastic! It was warm, the air was clean, and the people in Ecuador are so generous. These people were poor, yet they'd give you the shirt off their back if you needed it.

MICHELLE. I'm glad to hear that you and Vernon had such a great time. *(Pause.)* Did you miss me?

DAVE. *(He takes her in his arms.)* I missed you so much. I really missed the way you cradle me as I fall asleep.

(They kiss.)

MICHELLE. I missed you too. *(Seductively.)* I've got a special surprise for you tonight. *(They make out a bit. Then she stops.)* Not until tonight mister. How was the conference?

DAVE. Oh you know how it is. A bunch of pseudo intellectual blowhards droning on and on about Byron, Wordsworth, and Shelly. None of these guys knew what they were talking about. I mean, everyone knows that Byron was the greatest romantic poet. *(Pause.)* Anyway, how's work been?

MICHELLE. I'm defending this guy who's a total jerk. Every time I have a meeting with him he makes these creepy sexual advances like flicking his tongue at me like this. *(She makes the gesture with her tongue then she does a line of coke.)* And whenever I tell him to stop he's like:

"I'm sorry but you're just so beautiful." I'll tell you. If he keeps it up I'm going to make sure that he goes to jail for a very long time. See, what these guys don't realize is that I can be saying one thing and implying another through my gestures. I can say "My client is completely innocent" and then wink at the judge. Or I can make it clear through the tone in my voice that I don't actually believe anything I'm saying about his innocence.

DAVE. What's he accused of?

MICHELLE. Strangling some chick and then raping her corpse.

DAVE. Oh my god! That's sick!

MICHELLE. Tell me about it.

DAVE. Do you think he did it?

MICHELLE. Oh yeah. He did it. You should have seen the photos from the crime scene. Really gruesome stuff. He carved weird symbols into her skin and cut the webbing between her fingers. I'll tell you. That motherfucker better stop flicking his tongue at me or I'm gonna make sure he goes to jail for life! *(Pause.)* How was the coke in Ecuador?

DAVE. Oh yeah. It was amazing. Amazing. I brought you a little present. *(He takes a wrapped gift out of his suitcase.)* She opens it. It is an ounce of cocaine.

MICHELLE. Thank you honey! This is so sweet!

(They kiss. Then they greedily do some coke.)

End Scene

Scene Seven

(At rise DAVE and VERNON are in DAVE's Office.)

VERNON. How's the hangover?

DAVE. Moderate. On a scale of one to ten mine's a four. How about you?

VERNON. Mine's about a two and a half.

DAVE. Not bad. How much did you drink last night?

PURITY

VERNON. Abut a third of a liter of Johnnie Walker. How about you?

DAVE. Half a liter. *(Pause.)* Hey. I got the pictures developed.

VERNON. Where?

DAVE. I took them to the guy who tipped us off about Ecuador. *(Dave takes the pictures out of his desk. They look at the pictures.)* That was some sweet pussy wasn't it?

VERNON. *(Sweetly.)* The best. I miss her. I miss the games of hide and go seek that we played.

DAVE. Look at this one. You can't even see my dick because it's so far down her throat. That girl sure knew how to relax those gag muscles.

VERNON. *(Sweetly.)* Cumming in her mouth was the best feeling I've ever had.

DAVE. I liked cumming in her ass. I feel a little bad about making her bleed.

VERNON. I can't stop thinking about her. I'm in love with her Dave.

DAVE. Yeah. You're in love with her.

VERNON. I'm serious Dave!

DAVE. I'm serious too! She was just some good pussy. I mean. what do you think you're going to do? Bring her to America, divorce your wife, and make her your child bride?

VERNON. I loved the smell of her dark hair. I loved her soft skin, her smooth pussy. I want to adopt her Dave.

DAVE. What? How much coke have you done today?

VERNON. It could work! I'll convince Lisa that we'd be really good people if we adopted a poor Ecuadorian child. Think about it Think about all the organizations like Save The Children and Feed The Poor Dirty Children In Africa and Latin America. The world is overpopulated blah blah blah. It could work and then I'd have her all to myself.

DAVE. What are you going to do when she grows up?

VERNON. I'll do a Woody Allen. Everything worked out fine for him.

DAVE. Listen to me Vernon. You need to get this girl out of your head. You have a wife who loves and supports you. Let this little girl go.

VERNON. Can I keep the pictures?

DAVE. I'll make you a set after I have someone air brush our faces out of them so that we can sell them.

VERNON. O.K.

(There is a knock at DAVE's door.)

DAVE. Hold on a second! *(He puts away the pictures.)* Come in. *(Carl enters. He is an African American man dressed in Kente cloth and a Dashiki.)* Hey Carl!

CARL. Hey Dave!

DAVE. *(To VERNON.)* I just hired Carl to be one of the new Assistant Professors in the department.

VERNON. *(With no enthusiasm.)* Oh. That's great.

DAVE. And Vernon's a full professor and a good friend.

CARL. *(They shake hands.)* Nice to meet you.

VERNON. Nice to meet you too. What's your scholarly expertise?

CARL. African American Literature.

VERNON. Ah. I see. Very interesting.

CARL. What's yours?

VERNON. Romantic literature.

CARL. That's a good field.

VERNON. What's your favorite book?

CARL. The Autobiography Of Malcolm X.

VERNON. *(Genuinely.)* Does that really count as literature?

PURITY

CARL. Why wouldn't it be?
VERNON. Well, you know.

(Pause.)

CARL. No. I don't know.
DAVE. I have an idea! Why don't we invite Carl over to have
dinner with us and our wives on Saturday night!
VERNON. We could do that.
DAVE. Well Carl?
CARL. I'd love to.

End Scene

Scene Eight

(At rise VERNON, LISA, CARL, And MICHELLE are having drink
after dinner at DAVE's house. When the light's come up every
one is laughing except VERNON.)

LISA. So, where did you grow up?
CARL. Newark, New Jersey.
MICHELLE. Newark's a pretty rough place, isn't it?
CARL. Yeah. It was tough. My mom raised us by herself an
we lived in the projects.
LISA. How terrible for you! Where was your father?
CARL. In jail. He died there. My mom had me when she wa
sixteen years old. My dad was a drug dealer. He got caught wit

eight ounces of cocaine.

DAVE. *(In disbelief.)* They threw him in jail for life! Just for having eight ounces! I've bought- That sounds like racism to me!

MICHELLE. That is racist!

LISA. Totally. *(VERNON sighs loudly. Everyone looks at him for a moment. Pause.)* Honey? Don't you think what happened to Carl's father is racist?

VERNON. I think that people's actions have consequences.

CARL. That's true.

VERNON. I mean if you deal drugs and have children when you're a teenager, what do you think your life is going to be like?

LISA. Vernon stop!

CARL. *(To LISA.)* It's O.K. *(To VERNON.)* It's true that actions have consequences, but don't you think there is a sociological problem in the black community that leads to teenage pregnancy and drug addiction?

VERNON. No I don't think that. I think people in the ghetto are lazy and adverse to doing hard work. Instead of working hard in school and going to college they decide to deal drugs because it's easy money. They bring it upon themselves.

CARL. How can you say that?

VERNON. How can you say that it's a sociological problem?

CARL. Because I lived it! That's how. Where did you grow up?

VERNON. Short Hills.

CARL. Where did you go to high school?

VERNON. Pingry.

CARL. Oh I see. You're just a rich boy who never had to worry about anything. You can't understand the problems of the ghetto because you were born with a silver spoon in your mouth!

VERNON. That's not true! Sure we had money. Sure we belonged to a country club. The same one as Dave-

DAVE. Don't bring me into this.

VERNON. But I worked my butt off in school, studying for

four hours a night so that I could get into Harvard. I earned it.

CARL. You didn't earn anything. It was all handed to you. How is a child in the ghetto supposed to do well in school when his mother is on crack, his dad is in jail, and he's in an inner city classroom with forty kids and the teacher can't even control the class? In order to do well in school you need to live in an environment that is conducive to learning. And you need guidance. You had your parents to help you do your homework. You had a spacious room in a comfortable environment. These kids don't have their parents to help them! These kids live in two room apartments with no electricity and not even enough food to eat!

VERNON. You're exaggerating!

CARL. No I'm not. I lived it. I was happy if momma was able to feed us one meal a day!

VERNON. But you made it! You grew up in the ghetto and now you have a P.hD. If you can do it then any of these kids can do it. These kids use their environment as an excuse to justify their behavior. That's all I'm saying.

CARL. I was lucky.

VERNON. No you weren't! You got where you are because of hard work.

CARL. Look, all I'm saying is that there is a cycle of poverty that black people in the ghetto are stuck in. And until white society stops blaming black people for the violence and drugs, and realizes that resources need to be put into reducing class size and offering economic opportunity, then nothing is ever going to change.

LISA. I think you might be the racist Vernon. I agree with Carl's point of view.

MICHELLE. Me too.

DAVE. Me three.

End Scene

Scene Nine

(At rise VERNON is onstage alone addressing the audience.)

VERNON. What the fuck was that?

(Mimicking his wife.)

"I think you might be the racist Vernon"

Well so what if I'm a racist! They're all racists too. They just pretend to care about black people because Kente Cloth Carl was there.

(Mimicking Them.)

"We love Carl. Oh poor Carl had to grow up in the ghetto and he was raised by a single mom. Poor him"

I really hate that nigger! I mean, don't you hate niggers like that? Niggers who walk around wearing Kente Cloth and a Dashiki celebrating Kwanzaa and lecturing people about the plight of Ghetto life.

I'm sick of it! Aren't you?

We need to lead a revolution against these Kente Cloth niggers! I think we should round them up like Hitler rounded up the Jews!

He thinks he's so great because he went to Howard university. They call Howard the black Harvard. Well I went to the real Harvard! People go to Nigger Harvard because they're too stupid to get into the real one. We should burn Howard and all the rest of

PURITY

those Nigger Colleges too!

I hate Carl. Entering my White haven and turning my precious white friends against me. I was so happy. Do you know how hard I worked to surround myself with white people?

It's really hard when you're whole family is black! But I did it because I didn't want to be around niggers anymore.

Do you know how much I love my lily white wife? My white best friend?

How I love living every day knowing that that white woman is mine? All mine. It's status for me. When people see me walking down the street with my white best friend and my white wife, they know I'm different.

They say to themselves: "Ahh. He's not one of those dangerous gun wielding ghetto negroes! He's the kind of negro that I like! The kind of negro that I'd like to have over for dinner to show that I'm not a racist. The kind of negro that I just might let my daughter date."

A negro who's not going to go around quoting Malcolm X and exploiting my white guilt like Kente Cloth Carl.

End Of Scene

PURITY

Scene Ten

(At rise VERNON walks into DAVE's office. DAVE is working at his computer.)

VERNON. What's up?

DAVE. You know. What's up with you?

VERNON. Not much. How's your hangover?

DAVE. I'd say a three out of ten.

VERNON. *(Impressed with how mild DAVE's hangover is.)* Not bad! How much did you drink?

DAVE. About a third of a liter.

VERNON. Very Moderate.

DAVE. How's your hangover?

VERNON. About a six.

DAVE. That kind of sucks.

VERNON. Yeah. I drank half a liter.

DAVE. Half a liter's no good. You need a drink.

(DAVE pours VERNON a drink.)

VERNON. Why did you side with Carl the other night?

DAVE. What was I supposed to do?

VERNON. You're my best friend. You could have defended me!

DAVE. Defend you and look like a racist! No way! If I took your side Carl would tell every professor in the department that I'm a fucking racist. I'd lose my job.

VERNON. Do you think I'm a racist for the views I hold?

DAVE. Of course not! I feel the same way! But you can't go around saying things like that in front of black people.

VERNON. I'm black!

VERNON is flattered that DAVE thinks he's almost white. DAVE takes out a mirror with cocaine on it.)

VERNON. *(He does a line.)* Thanks.

DAVE. Check this out! I uploaded all of our pictures of Maria and created a website!

VERNON. You what?

DAVE. Dude. We're going to make so much money.

VERNON. We can't do this. We're going to get caught. The FBI's always arresting people for doing this kind of shit.

DAVE. Don't worry about it. I had my friend hook it up so that no one can trace it back to our computers! How cool is that?

VERNON. You're exploiting her!

DAVE. What?

VERNON. Yeah. You heard me. You're exploiting my little girl!

DAVE. Vernon. You're really starting to worry me. You need to come back to earth. Maria is not your little girl and you exploited her just as much as I did when you fucked her.

VERNON. I didn't exploit her! It was love!

DAVE. It was not love. She just had a really tight pussy. That's what you loved. Nothing more. I've got to go teach. Are you going to be O.K?

VERNON. Yeah.

DAVE. *(He starts to leave.)* Oh yeah. Can you take a look at this book? *(Hands VERNON the book.)* It's called: "A Heartbreaking Work Of Staggering Genius." It was nominated for the Pulitzer a couple of years ago. I'm thinking about making it required reading for freshman comp.

VERNON. Yeah. I'll take a look at it.

DAVE. Thanks.

(He leaves.)

End Scene

PURITY

Scene Eleven

(Fantasy Sequence #1. VERNON is still standing in DAVE's office when MARIA runs onstage wearing Lingerie.)

MARIA. Hi daddy!

VERNON. *(Picks her up and kisses her on the lips.)* How's daddy's little girl? *(He puts her into his lap.)* What did you learn in school today?

MARIA. I learned that George Washington was a good man because he didn't tell any lies. When his father asked whether he had chopped down a cherry tree he told the truth.

VERNON. That's a good lesson honey. Honesty is always the best policy. Promise me that you'll never tell lies.

MARIA. I promise. I never will!

Daddy. There's something hard in your pants.

VERNON. Honey. Would you mind moving your butt back and forth in daddy's lap? That would make daddy very happy.

(She starts to grind her butt into his lap.)

MARIA. Like this daddy?

VERNON. Yes Maria. Just like that.

MARIA. Oh daddy. You're getting harder. It feels so good.

VERNON. I'm getting harder because I love you. This is how a father shows his daughter love.

MARIA. I'm getting all wet between my legs daddy.

VERNON. That's natural honey. That's what happens when your daddy loves you.

MARIA. Do I feel good daddy?

VERNON. Like heaven.

MARIA. Am I making my daddy feel good? All I want is to

make my daddy feel good. *(She has an orgasm.)* Oh Daddy.
    VERNON. Oh Maria. My little angel Maria.

(LISA ENTERS wearing lingerie.)

    LISA. *(Seductive anger.)* What are you two doing? *(They stop.)*
Were you starting without me? I told you not to get started without
me. Vernon?
    VERNON. Yes dear.
    LISA. Do you love our daughter more than you love me?
    VERNON. Of course not honey. I love you both the same.
(VERNON and LISA kiss for a few moments then stop.) And does
Marie love her mommy?
    MARIA. Very much.

(LISA kisses MARIA on the lips. LISA and VERNON start to make
out while MARIA starts to give VERNON a blow job as the lights
fade to black.)

End Scene

Scene Twelve

(At rise VERNON is addressing his freshman English class.)

    VERNON. I read your papers and I was very disappointed to
find that many of you don't know how to write in proper formal
essay structure. This is something that you should have mastered in

high school. As a matter of fact I'm amazed that you were able to gain acceptance into a prestigious institution like this without knowing how to write properly. I mean, you had to submit an essay to get in. So listen up freshman, I'm only going to say this once. An essay has three parts: The introduction, the body, and the conclusion. In the first sentence of your introductory paragraph you must introduce the text you're writing about and the author. You must underline or italize the the title of the text. The last sentence of your introductory paragraph should contain your thesis. Your thesis presents the topic that you will argue in your paper. The first sentence of each body paragraph is your topic sentence. Your topic sentence states what that particular paragraph is about. Your paper should never stray from your thesis and a body paragraph should never stray from it's topic sentence.

Focus must be maintained at all times! You must include two quotes from the text in each body paragraph. When you quote you must use parenthetical notation.

In the first sentence of your conclusion you must re-state your thesis. In the conclusion you must summarize the major points that you made in the essay. The conclusion is also the time to give a personal example from your life or the world.

I don't want to see the word I anywhere else in your paper! You don't say "I think Iago is in love with Desdemona!" you say "Iago is in love with Desdemona!" The latter is a much stronger statement. The second you say "I think" your credibility is called into question.

If I see the word I anywhere but the conclusion you will automatically receive an F. If anyone hands in a paper that's not written in the exact manner that I have proscribed you will automatically fail!

Remember to write all your papers in 12 point font Times New Roman. None of that Courier New business.

You're Dismissed.

End Scene

Scene Thirteen

(At rise MICHELLE, CARL, and LISA are alone talking in VERNON and LISA's home.)

CARL. And that's how my Great Great Grandfather got shot trying to escape from slavery.

MICHELLE. That's horrible Carl!

LISA. Your poor Great Great Grandfather!

MICHELLE. Will you tell us another story about your ancestry?

CARL. I don't know. I feel like I'm boring you.

LISA. Not at all. Nothing could be further from the truth.

MICHELLE. We love hearing your stories!

CARL. O.K. My Great Great Grandmother on my mother's side was a great beauty. They say that she was the most beautiful slave on Mr. Higgins plantation. Everyone was in love with her. Even Mr. Higgins, her owner. Every night Mr. Higgins would sneak out of bed after his wife had gone to sleep and he would crawl into my

Great Great Grandmother's shack and rape her.

LISA. How do you know it was rape?

CARL. Well, she didn't have much choice in the matter, now did she?

LISA. I suppose not. Sorry for interrupting.

CARL. Anyway, my Great Great Grandmother had a boyfriend on another plantation. She would sneak off at night after Mr. Higgins had returned to his great big house. But Mr. Higgins caught wind of this and became very jealous. One night after he had raped my Great Great Grandmother he told her that she better not go anywhere that night and then he left. She disobeyed him and snuck off to see her boyfriend anyway. When Mr. Higgins found her missing later that night a blinding rage overtook him. He could not bear the thought of my Great Great Grandmother with another man. The next morning after Mr. Higgins ate his breakfast and said his morning prayers he used to pray for a half hour each morning. he called her out from the field and tied her to the whipping post. He gave her 100 lashes all the while shouting "Nigger Bitch" and "Nigger Whore" as his wife looked on. They say her blood ran like a river when it was all over.

LISA. Oh my god. Slavery was so terrible for your people. How could he do that in front of his wife? I mean she must have known.

CARL. That's just the way things were then. It was common practice. Do you want to know something else?

MICHELLE. What?

CARL. Mr. Higgins the man who whipped my Great Great Grandmother and raped her every night is my Great Great Grandfather on my mother's side.

MICHELLE. Oh my god! How does that make you feel?

CARL. I don't know. I have very complicated feelings about the matter. I guess in reality I'm part slave owner and part slave. I wish I destroy my white slave owning blood. But I can't. I can't. It's just as much a part of me as my blackness.

PURITY

(He starts to cry. MICHELLE and LISA comfort him be showering him with kisses all the while repeating "Poor Carl, Poor Carl",

(He stops crying.)

LISA. We should go soon. Vernon's going to be home any minute.

MICHELLE. We can go to my place. Dave won't be home for a couple of hours.

End Scene

Scene Fourteen

(At rise CARL is having sex with MICHELLE from behind while LISA watches and masturbates.)

CARL. Oh yeah. C'mon baby. Say it! *(More forcefully.)* Say it!
MICHELLE. Fuck me Ghetto Nigger!
CARL. Again!
MICHELLE. Fuck me you Ghetto Nigger!
CARL. Good. Good. You're a dirty white bitch. You know that? Say the next thing! Say it!
MICHELLE. Pull my hair you jungle monkey! Pull my hair! *(CARL Pulls her hair.)* Harder!

(He pulls her hair harder.)

CARL. That's right you stupid white whore. Say the next thing!
MICHELLE. I don't remember.

(MICHELLE has an orgasm.)

CARL. Try harder. I'm almost there!
MICHELLE. Your dick feels so good.
CARL. No! That's not it!

(LISA has an orgasm.)

MICHELLE. Oh yeah, Fuck me like a run away slave!
CARL. Oh yeah!

(He ejaculates.)

LISA. It's not true that all black men have big dicks. Your dick is so much bigger than Vernon's.
CARL. It's your turn you horny white slut.

(LISA and MICHELLE switch places and CARL starts to have sex with LISA as the lights fade to black.)

End Scene

PURITY

Scene Fifteen

(At rise VERNON has just walked into DAVE's office.)

DAVE. Hey Vern. What's up?

VERNON. There's something strange going on.

DAVE. What do you mean?

VERNON. I came home the other day and Carl was hanging out with Michelle and Lisa. Isn't that weird?

DAVE. It is a little weird. I think they feel sorry for him. The really seem to be into his ghetto upbringing and plight as a black man.

VERNON. I know. What are we going to do?

DAVE. Do?

VERNON. Yeah. What are we going to do?

DAVE. Why do we have to do anything? I mean, it seems pretty harmless. Besides, I like Carl. It really doesn't bother me that much. Did you get a chance to read "A Heartbreaking Work Of Staggering Genius?"

VERNON. Yeah.

DAVE. What did you think?

VERNON. I think it's good. His writing is pretty innovative. Instead of telling a linear story he writes in the way that the human brain actually functions. Making random associations and delving into random pieces of distant memory. It's very sophisticated stuff.

DAVE. I agree. Do you think it's a good book for freshman comp?

VERNON. I think it's a great book for that. The students will think it's interesting and I was thinking that we could have them write their own memoirs after they've read the book.

DAVE. That's brilliant! They'll read a memoir and write their own!

VERNON. Yeah. Their memoirs will be much more interesting

to read than those boring papers written in formal essay structure. It's so fucking boring. Dude. Can't you make a rule that senior professors don't have to teach freshman comp? I really hate it.

DAVE. We all hate it, but there's nothing that I can do. This is the way the president wants it.

VERNON. But Senior Professors at other university's don't have to teach the lower level writing classes. They get to teach what they want!

DAVE. I know. I know, but the president feels that freshman should have access to the real professors, not just adjuncts and grad students. He thinks it's a more egalitarian system.

VERNON. That's pure bullshit.

DAVE. I know. Hey. This is for you.

(DAVE takes five thousand dollars out of a drawer and hands it to VERNON.)

VERNON. What's this for?

DAVE. It's from our internet site. The pictures of Maria are selling like hotcakes dude!

VERNON. Really? How much are you selling the pictures for?

DAVE. Thirty five dollars each and four for one hundred.

VERNON. Jesus Christ. How much is this?

DAVE. Five thousand dollars. I think we should go back and take more pictures!

VERNON. I don't think so, and I don't want this money.

DAVE. Why?

VERNON. You know why.

DAVE. Not this sissy bullshit again!

VERNON. I know you think it's weird, but I refuse to exploit her anymore. I love her.

(He gives the money back to DAVE.)

DAVE. I'm not going to fight you on this one. More money for me.

VERNON. Why don't you buy me an ounce of cocaine for my birthday and we'll call it even.

DAVE. Deal.

End Scene

Scene Sixteen

(At rise VERNON is on stage alone addressing the audience.)

VERNON. What the fuck is going on? It's bad enough that Carl exists. But now he's hanging out with my women! My white women! No-siree-bob. I don't like it one bit. There's something fishy about the whole situation.

He wants to fuck my women. I know it! He wants to steal my beautiful white goddesses away from me. He doesn't understand white women the way I understand white women. He doesn't know how to cherish and treat them like the beautiful gems that they are. He's probably never even slept with a white woman. He's not good enough to sleep with a white woman. White women don't like ghetto dashiki wearing niggers like Carl!

Can you believe that he's a professor? Can you believe that some university actually gave him a Phd? For what? Reading Malcolm

PURITY

X?

Can you believe that your children might have him as a teacher someday? Do you want your children to be alone in a classroom with him? I certainly don't.

I love Dave's wife. I never meant to sleep with her but it just happens sometimes. You know. The first time it happened we were at a party, Dave and Lisa couldn't make it, and every word we said to one another was filled with sexual tension. I mean, we couldn't control ourselves, so we went into the master bedroom of our friends apartment, locked the door, and fucked like I was going out of style. And you know what the best thing is? She loves to get fucked in the ass! SHE LOVES IT!

My wife won't let me fuck her in the ass. So if you really think about it it's not really cheating. When I fuck my wife I fuck her vagina and when I fuck Michelle it's usually in her ass. Is anal sex really sex?

I actually hear that some girls have anal sex to prevent losing their virginity. I wish I had dated a girl like that in high school.

I don't want you to get the impression that I'm fucking my best friend's wife behind his back. I don't fuck her that much and I don't go out of my way to do it. It just happens sometimes. You know?

Carl better stay away from my alabaster queens or else there's going to be trouble.

End Scene

PURITY

Scene Seventeen

*(Fantasy sequence #2. At rise VERNON is alone on stage and there
is a Magic Lamp on the floor. VERNON picks up the Magic
Lamp and rubs it. A GENIE appears.)*

GENIE. Hello.
VERNON. Uh Hi.
GENIE. What's your name?
VERNON. Vernon.
GENIE. Vernon, I'm going to grant you three wishes.
VERNON. What should I wish for?
GENIE. You can wish for anything that your heart desires.
VERNON. Anything?
GENIE. Yes anything.
VERNON. My first wish is to be white.

(The GENIE applies white makeup to VERNON's face.)

GENIE. Your wish has been granted. What's your second wish?
VERNON. I want to be a southern plantation owner.

(The stage is transformed into a southern plantation.)

GENIE. Your wish has been granted. What's your final wish?
VERNON. I want Kente Cloth Carl to be my slave.

*(CARL ENTERS wearing tattered slave clothing. LISA ENTERS as
a southern belle. VERNON smokes a cigar.)*

CARL. Massa, you wanted to see me?
VERNON. Are you looking directly at me? You put your head

PURITY

down and avert your eyes when you're in the presence of a white man. You understand?

CARL. Yes massa. I'm sorry massa.

VERNON. Good. Now go fetch me another Mint Julep nigger.

CARL. Yes Massa.

(CARL EXITS.)

VERNON. How's my beautiful peach today?

LISA. I'm doing just fine. My nigresses have been making me a new quilt! I can't wait for it to be finished. The only problem is that niggers work so slow sometimes.

VERNON. A truer sentence has never been spoken. Take Carl for instance. *(He shouts.)* Nigger! Hurry up with my Mint Julep! I'm thirsty!

LISA. Now you musn't get angry Vernon. Carl can't help it. Being lazy and shiftless is just their nature.

VERNON. I know, but I feel as an upstanding white people it is our duty to rid niggers of their animalistic and lazy nature. Now you watch what I do to Carl when he gets back. I'm going to show you how to encourage niggers to stop being so niggerlike.

(CARL ENTERS running with VERNON's Mint Julep.)

CARL. I'm sorry it took so long massa.

(He hands VERNON the drink.)

VERNON. You spilled some when you ran in. You must learn to be more careful. I paid good money for this liquor and I don't like to see it wasted. Do you like to waste money boy?

CARL. No massa.

VERNON. Good. Now lick up what you spilled.

CARL. But Massa-

VERNON. Don't talk back boy!

CARL. But massa-

VERNON. Lick it up nigger! *(CARL licks up what he spilled. VERNON takes a sip of his Mint Julep.)* How did it taste?

CARL. That's a good drink massa.

VERNON. If you think this is good then you have very bad taste. Come here. *(CARL walks over to VERNON. VERNON throws his drink into CARL's face.)* There ain't enough Julep in this drink! Now go quickly! Make me another one with more Julep! *(CARL runs offstage. He turns to LISA.)* Now that's how you teach niggers to stop being so niggerlike.

LISA. You did a good job honey. I wish I could learn to treat niggers like that, then my life would be so much easier. I bet my niggresses would've already finished my quilt if I treated them correctly, like you do.

VERNON. You can do it! You just need to be more firm. Your problem is that you sometimes treat niggers like they're human.

LISA. How dare you say that top me?! I certainly do not treat niggers like they're human.

VERNON. Honey, I'm not trying to insult you. I'm just trying to offer some constructive criticism. For instance, sometimes I hear you address niggers by their name. I always address them as nigger or boy or girl in the case of a woman.

LISA. I'd like to do that but how will they know who you're talking to? I mean, whenever I walk into a room and say "Nigger" they all turn around. How will niggers know which nigger I'm talking to if I don't use their name?

VERNON. Hmm. That's an interesting question. You know, I never thought about it like that. I'll have to sleep on it. *(CARL ENTERS walking very slowly and carefully so that he doesn't spill any*

PURITY

of the drink.) You are such a slow nigger. That took even longer than last time!

CARL. Sorry massa. I wanted to make it jus right for you. *(He hands VERNON the drink. VERNON takes a sip.)* How is it massa?

VERNON. *(VERNON takes another sip. He rolls the liquor around in his mouth for awhile assessing the quality of the drink.)* You've done a good job boy! This is a fine Mint Julep!

(LISA has a coughing fit and VERNON and CARL look at LISA. VERNON pats her on the back to try and alleviate the coughing.)

CARL. Do you want me to fetch you some water Ma'am?

(VERNON looks up and sees that CARL is looking at his wife.)

VERNON. *(Stares at CARL in disbelief for a couple of moments.)* How dare you look at my wife? How dare you? Your eyes should never gaze upon a white woman's face. Never. I can see it in your eyes. You're lusting after my wife! Do you actually think that a white woman could ever be attracted to a monkey like you? All you niggers are the same. Your most sacred wish is to rape a white woman. That's what you would so all day if we didn't keep you in your places. I'm going to whip that fantasy out of your head you nappy headed ashy nigger! *(He roughly strings CARL up to the whipping post.)* This is going to teach you you filthy rapist!

(He whips CARL seven times. After each lash CARL let's out an excruciating scream. VERNON whips him with manic joy.)

End scene

PURITY

Scene Eighteen

(At rise DAVE has frantically entered VERNON's office.)

DAVE. Dude, you were right. There's something really fucked up about the situation with Carl and our wives.

VERNON. What happened?

DAVE. You don't want to know. I'm so disgusted. I don't even want to say it.

VERNON. What? You have to tell me!

DAVE. I went home this afternoon and they were having a fucking orgy!

VERNON. Please tell me you're kidding.

DAVE. I'm dead serious. He was fucking your wife while my wife watched and masturbated. And she was saying all this weird shit like fuck me you ghetto nigger.

VERNON. He was fucking my wife?

DAVE. Are you fucking deaf? Yes, he was fucking your wife.

VERNON. What did you do?

DAVE. Nothing.

VERNON. Did they see you?

DAVE. No. I just walked out. I was in shock.

VERNON. What should we do?

DAVE. I have no clue. The situation is just so crazy. I mean what do they see in him? He's so ugly! He's got those fucking dreadlocks.

VERNON. Fire him! You have to fire him.

DAVE. I can't fire him dude. He was just hired.

VERNON. Well, something needs to be done about that motherfucker.

DAVE. Yeah.

VERNON. I'll take care of it.

PURITY

DAVE. What are you going to do?

VERNON. Don't worry about it. I've got to go.

DAVE. I shut down the website.

VERNON. Why?

DAVE. It was taking up too much of my time. At the rate I was going, I would've had to quit my job and become a professional pornographer.

(He laughs awkwardly.)

VERNON. *(Confused.)* O.K.

(Lights Down.)

End Scene

Scene Nineteen

(At rise VERNON is tying a noose to a tree branch in CARL's backyard. He then breaks into CARL's house where CARL is sleeping. VERNON creeps up to CARL's bed with a gun. VERNON pulls up a chair and watches CARL Sleep for awhile with the gun pointed at him.)

VERNON. Rise and shine! *(CARL remains sleeping.)* C'mon! Rise and shine Carl. There's African drumming at the Alvin Ailey center. Don't you want to see some black people dance and beat drums like monkeys?

CARL. *(He wakes up. Startled.)* What's going on?

VERNON. I thought we could go see the African Drummers at the Alvin Ailey center.

CARL. Am I dreaming?

VERNON. This is no dream.

CARL. What time is it?

VERNON. Three o'clock in the morning?

CARL. *(Notices the gun.)* Why do you have that gun?

VERNON. It's for protection. I hear this neighborhood is pretty violent. Lot's of black people I hear.

CARL. You're scaring me.

VERNON. When did I start to scare you? You seem pretty fearless to me. Turn over.

CARL. What for?

VERNON. Turn over or I'm going to fucking shoot you. *(He slaps CARL across the face.)* Carl turns onto his stomach. *(VERNON straddles him and ties his hands together.)* Good boy.

CARL. Why are you doing this to me?

VERNON. I hear you like white women.

CARL. *(Silence.)*

VERNON. What? Cat got your tongue.

CARL. Look Vernon. It's not what you think.

VERNON. Really? Fucking my wife isn't what I think it is? O.K. Then tell me what it is.

CARL. Look man, she seduced me.

VERNON. Don't you mean "They" seduced you?! Don't forget that you fucked Dave's wife too. I thought you'd have some respect for the man who gave you a job.

CARL. O.K. They seduced me. They took advantage of me. Hey Brother. The flesh is weak. I didn't know what to do.

VERNON. You're a real coward. You know that? When I first met you I thought you were an upstanding, moral, righteous, black

PURITY

guy. I actually kind of admired you. I didn't like you. But I admire people who have morals and values because I have no concept of what that's like. I thought that maybe you were a better person than me. But now I know that you're as guilty as the rest of us. We're all going to have a big party in hell! Yeah!

CARL. Please Vernon.

VERNON. Get the fuck up! *(CARL doesn't move.)* I said get the fuck up you stupid nigger!

(CARL gets up. He is only wearing his underwear.)

CARL. Can I put on some clothes?

VERNON. No. you look great in your underwear you sexy bitch. *(VERNON grabs CARL's butt and licks his face.)* I see why my women like you so much. Ohh. Ohh. You're so sexy! Makes me feel gay! Makes me want to stick my dick in your ass! Yeeeha!

(VERNON licks CARL's face as he presses the gun into CARL's chest.)

CARL. Where are you taking me?

VERNON. Into your backyard. I've got a big surprise for you. Walk faster you oversexed nigger! You know, I didn't think a Dashiki wearing Kente cloth nigger like you would've been interested in white she-devils.

CARL. *(They are at the rope. Very scared.)* Why are you doing his to me?

VERNON. Do you really want to know?

CARL. Yes.

VERNON. First put your head through the rope. Then I'll tell ou. *(Climbs up onto the stepstool.)* Oh Carl. You smell pretty bad. Don't tell me that you shit yourself. *(CARL jumps off of the stepstool nd starts to run across the stage. VERNON shoots him and he falls.)*

PURITY

That'll teach you to try to escape from me you stupid nigger. *(Pause.* I hope that tainting my white doves was worth it for you, because they'll never be the same to me. A dark stain now rests upon them.

(VERNON calmly walks offstage.)

End Of Play

ABOUT THE PLAYWRIGHT

Thomas Bradshaw's play entitled *Purity* was produced at Performance Space 122 in January 2007 and his plays *Strom Thurmond Is Not A Racist* and *Cleansed* were produced on a double bill at The Brick Theatre in February '07. *Strom/Cleansed* have been nominated for Outstanding Original Full Length Script by the 2007 New York Innovative Theater Awards. He has been featured in *The New York Times*, as one of *Time Out New York's* ten playwrights to watch, and as one of *Paper Magazine's* 2006 Beautiful People. His play entitled *Prophet* was presented at P.S. 122 in December 2005. *Strom Thurmond Is Not A Racist* won The American Theater Coop's 2005 National Playwriting Contest. He was a fellow at New York Theater Workshop in '06 -'07 and has been a member of Soho Rep's Writer/Director Lab as well as Lincoln Center's. He performed in the premiere of Richard Maxwell's *The End Of Reality* at The Kitchen in January 2006 and he performed in Young Jean Lee's *Pullman, WA* at P.S. 122 in March 2005. He performed throughout Europe with *The End Of Reality* in the fall of '06. He received his MFA from Mac Wellman's playwriting program and is a Professor at Brooklyn College. Thomas is also the recipient of a 2006 Jerome Foundation Grant.

Also by
Thomas Bradshaw...

Cleansed

Dawn

Purity

Southern Promises

Strom Thurmond is Not a Racist

OTHER TITLES AVAILABLE FROM SAMUEL FRENCH

SOUTHERN PROMISES

Thomas Bradshaw

Drama / 6m, 2f, with doubling / Simple Set
When the master of the plantation dies, he wills his slaves to be freed, but his wife doesn't think that good property should be squandered. Pandemonium ensues. The play is inspired by the true story of Henry Box Brown who escaped to the north by mailing himself in a box. *Southern Promises* provides a unique portrait of the old south.

Bradshaw was named "Playwright of the Year" by the theater blog KUL-That Sounds Cool and *Southern Promises* was named among the best performances of Stage and Screen for 2008 in *The New Yorker.*

"Slowly, almost single-handedly, a twenty-eight-year-old black playwright named Thomas Bradshaw has been taking on the idea of race in the theatre. At the same time, he has sliced open the pretensions of the white avant-garde with a wittily glistening axe. In his new play, *Southern Promises* (at Performance Space 122), one can catch a glimpse of Bradshaw's anarchic gifts."
—*The New Yorker*

"It's a striking, challenging piece that studies the abuse of power and the liquidity of morality."
—*NYTheatre.com*

"Likely to leave you speechless."
—*The New York Times*

CPSIA information can be obtained
at www.ICGtesting.com
Printed in the USA
BVHW04s1805080918
526911BV00002B/48/P

9 780573 650116